The Diplomat's Handbook

Mastering the Art of Managing a Malevolent Manager

By Khaled Bouajaja

Content:

1. Understanding Your Malicious Boss

The Different Types of Malicious Bosses

When it comes to dealing with a malicious boss, the first step is to understand who they are and what makes them tick. Malicious bosses can take many different forms, but by understanding their motivations and behaviors, you can better navigate the workplace and avoid potential pitfalls.

1.1 The Bully

One common type of malicious boss is the bully. These bosses use intimidation and aggression to get what they want. They may yell, belittle, or publicly humiliate employees to assert their dominance. Bullying behavior can have serious negative consequences on employee morale, productivity, and mental health.

To deal with a bullying boss, it's important to establish boundaries and hold them accountable for their behavior. Document any instances of bullying and report them to HR or a higher-up manager if necessary. Seek support from colleagues and consider speaking with a therapist to manage the emotional toll of working with a bully.

1.2 The Micromanager

Micromanagers are bosses who closely monitor and control their employees' work. They may second-guess decisions, require frequent updates, and refuse to delegate tasks. Micromanagers can stifle creativity and innovation, and make employees feel undervalued and untrusted.

To manage a micromanager, try to understand their need for control. Provide regular updates and anticipate their questions and concerns. Find ways to demonstrate your competence and build trust. If possible, try to negotiate for more autonomy and clear expectations.

1.3 The Passive-Aggressive Boss

Passive-aggressive bosses may appear pleasant and agreeable on the surface, but behind the scenes, they undermine and sabotage their employees. They may make sarcastic comments, withhold information, or create unreasonable expectations.

To handle a passive-aggressive boss, be direct and assertive. Clarify expectations and hold them accountable for their actions. Avoid getting pulled into their games or trying to appease them. Seek support from colleagues and document any instances of their behavior.

1.4 The Narcissist

Narcissistic bosses have an inflated sense of self-importance and a lack of empathy for others. They may demand constant attention and admiration, and disregard the needs and opinions of their employees. Narcissistic bosses can create a toxic work environment and cause significant damage to team dynamics.

To work with a narcissistic boss, try to avoid taking their behavior personally. Focus on your own work and goals, and seek feedback from others to maintain perspective. Set boundaries and avoid getting caught up in their drama. Consider seeking outside support from a therapist or coach to manage the emotional toll of working with a narcissist.

1.5 The Incompetent Boss

Incompetent bosses lack the skills, knowledge, or experience to effectively manage their team. They may make poor decisions, fail to communicate effectively, or struggle with basic tasks. Incompetent bosses can create frustration and confusion among their employees, and can negatively impact the success of the organization.

To handle an incompetent boss, try to be patient and supportive. Offer help and guidance when appropriate, but avoid taking on more than you can handle. Communicate clearly and seek clarity on expectations. Consider finding mentors or support outside the organization to build your own skills and confidence.

In summary, understanding the different types of malicious bosses is an important step in managing your career and navigating the workplace. By recognizing their behaviors and motivations, you can better anticipate challenges and develop effective strategies for success.

Identifying Your Boss's Triggers and Motivations

Once you've identified the type of malicious boss you're dealing with, the next step is to understand their triggers and motivations. By doing so, you can better anticipate their behavior and develop strategies for managing their actions. Here are some tips for identifying your boss's triggers and motivations:

2.1 Observe Their Behavior

One of the best ways to understand your boss's triggers and motivations is to observe their behavior. Take note of when they seem most stressed or irritable, and what events or circumstances seem to trigger their negative reactions. Similarly, pay attention to when they seem most engaged and motivated, and what activities or tasks seem to bring out their best work.

2.2 Ask for Feedback

Another way to gain insight into your boss's triggers and motivations is to ask for feedback. Ask them what they find most challenging or rewarding about their job, and what factors contribute to their success or frustration. Similarly, ask for feedback on your own work and how you can best support their goals.

2.3 Review Past Interactions

Review past interactions you've had with your boss to identify patterns in their behavior. Consider times when they've been particularly critical or supportive, and what events or circumstances may have contributed to their reactions. Similarly, review past projects or initiatives and identify what seemed to motivate or frustrate them.

2.4 Consider Their Personality

Your boss's personality can also provide clues to their triggers and motivations. Consider their communication style, work habits, and values. Do they prefer to work alone or collaborate with others? Are they motivated by recognition or autonomy? By understanding their personality, you can better anticipate their needs and preferences.

2.5 Review Organizational Goals

Finally, consider your organization's goals and priorities. Your boss's motivations are likely tied to the organization's mission and objectives. Consider how their role fits into the larger picture, and what factors may be driving their behavior. Similarly, consider how your own work contributes to the organization's success and how you can align your efforts with your boss's priorities.

In summary, identifying your boss's triggers and motivations requires careful observation, feedback, and reflection. By understanding what drives their behavior, you can better anticipate their needs and preferences and develop effective strategies for managing your interactions.

How Your Boss's Personal Life Affects Their Behavior at Work

It's no secret that our personal lives can have a significant impact on our behavior at work. This is true for everyone, including your boss. Understanding how your boss's personal life affects their behavior at work can help you develop strategies for managing their actions. Here are some ways your boss's personal life may impact their behavior:

3.1 Stress from Personal Issues

Personal issues such as relationship problems, financial troubles, or health concerns can all cause stress that spills over into the workplace. Your boss may be more irritable, short-tempered, or emotionally distant when dealing with these types of stressors. It's important to be empathetic and understanding in these situations while also setting boundaries to protect yourself and maintain a professional working relationship.

3.2 Health Concerns

Health concerns can also impact your boss's behavior at work. Chronic pain, mental health issues, and other health conditions can cause your boss to be more irritable, less productive, or less engaged. As with personal issues, it's important to be understanding and empathetic in these situations. Encourage your boss to seek professional help if needed, and offer support where appropriate.

3.3 Work-Life Balance

Your boss's work-life balance can also have a significant impact on their behavior. If your boss is working long hours, constantly checking their email, or otherwise failing to disconnect from work, they may be more stressed and less able to engage with you and other team members. Encourage your boss to prioritize self-care and to set boundaries around their work hours and communication.

3.4 Personality Traits

Some personality traits may also make your boss more susceptible to certain types of personal issues. For example, if your boss is a perfectionist, they may be more prone to burnout or anxiety. If they are an introvert, they may struggle with networking or public speaking. Understanding your boss's personality can help you anticipate their needs and preferences and adjust your communication style accordingly.

3.5 Positive Personal Experiences

It's also important to recognize that positive personal experiences can impact your boss's behavior at work. For example, if your boss is going through a particularly happy time in their personal life, such as getting married or having a child, they may be more engaged, energized, and optimistic. Encourage and celebrate these positive experiences with your boss to foster a positive work environment.

In conclusion, your boss's personal life can have a significant impact on their behavior at work. By understanding how personal issues, health concerns, work-life balance, personality traits, and positive experiences can impact your boss's behavior, you can develop effective strategies for managing your interactions and fostering a positive work environment.

2. Maintaining Your Composure

Developing Emotional Intelligence

Dealing with a malicious boss can be incredibly challenging, but maintaining your composure is key to managing your interactions effectively. Emotional intelligence is a critical skill for staying calm and professional in difficult situations. Here are some tips for developing emotional intelligence:

Understand Your Emotions

The first step in developing emotional intelligence is to understand your own emotions. Pay attention to how you're feeling, both physically and emotionally, and identify the specific emotions you're experiencing. Once you can recognize your emotions, you can learn to manage them more effectively.

Practice Self-Regulation

Self-regulation is the ability to manage your emotions and behavior in response to different situations. This includes things like taking a deep breath before responding to a difficult email, or reframing negative thoughts to be more positive. Practicing self-regulation can help you stay calm and composed in the face of difficult interactions.

Show Empathy

Empathy is the ability to understand and share the feelings of others. Showing empathy to your boss, even if they are being difficult, can help de-escalate the situation and create a more positive working relationship. Practice active listening, ask questions to understand your boss's perspective, and try to see things from their point of view.

Practice Mindfulness

Mindfulness is the practice of being present and fully engaged in the moment. Practicing mindfulness can help you stay focused on the present situation and avoid getting caught up in negative thoughts or emotions. Mindfulness can also help you develop a greater awareness of your own emotions and how they impact your behavior.

Seek Support

Dealing with a malicious boss can be incredibly stressful, and it's important to seek support when you need it. Talk to trusted friends or family members, or consider seeking out a therapist or counselor. Having a support system can help you manage your emotions and stay resilient in the face of difficult situations.

In conclusion, developing emotional intelligence is critical for maintaining your composure when dealing with a malicious boss. By understanding your own emotions, practicing self-regulation, showing empathy, practicing mindfulness, and seeking support, you can manage your interactions more effectively and create a more positive working relationship with your boss.

Staying Calm in High-Pressure Situations

Staying calm in high-pressure situations is a critical skill for anyone, but it's especially important when dealing with a malicious boss. Here are some strategies for staying calm and composed when the pressure is on:

Focus on Your Breathing

One of the most effective ways to stay calm in high-pressure situations is to focus on your breathing. Take slow, deep breaths in through your nose and out through your mouth. This can help slow your heart rate, lower your blood pressure, and reduce feelings of anxiety or stress.

Use Positive Self-Talk

Negative self-talk can be incredibly damaging in high-pressure situations, leading to feelings of anxiety and self-doubt. Instead, use positive self-talk to encourage yourself and stay motivated. Tell yourself things like "I can handle this" or "I've got this under control."

Stay Focused on the Task at Hand

It's easy to get overwhelmed in high-pressure situations, but staying focused on the task at hand can help you stay calm and composed. Break the task down into smaller, manageable steps, and focus on completing each one before moving on to the next.

Visualize Success

Visualization is a powerful tool for staying calm and confident in high-pressure situations. Imagine yourself successfully completing the task, or visualize a positive outcome. This can help you stay motivated and focused on your goals.

Take Breaks

When the pressure is on, it can be tempting to work non-stop until the task is complete. However, taking breaks can actually help you stay calm and focused. Take a few minutes to stretch, go for a walk, or do something else that relaxes you.

Practice Relaxation Techniques

Relaxation techniques such as meditation, yoga, or progressive muscle relaxation can also be helpful for staying calm in high-pressure situations. These techniques can help reduce muscle tension, lower your heart rate, and calm your mind.

Seek Support

Dealing with a malicious boss can be incredibly stressful, and it's important to seek support when you need it. Talk to trusted friends or family members, or consider seeking out a therapist or counselor. Having a support system can help you manage your emotions and stay resilient in the face of difficult situations.

In conclusion, staying calm in high-pressure situations is a critical skill for dealing with a malicious boss. By focusing on your breathing, using positive self-talk, staying focused on the task at hand, visualizing success, taking breaks, practicing relaxation techniques, and seeking support, you can manage your emotions and stay composed in even the most challenging situations.

Avoiding Confrontation

Avoiding confrontation can be an effective strategy for managing interactions with a malicious boss. Here are some tips for avoiding confrontation:

Choose Your Battles

Not every disagreement is worth pursuing. Choose your battles carefully, and focus on issues that are truly important. Letting go of minor issues can help you avoid unnecessary confrontation.

Stay Professional

Maintaining a professional demeanor is key to avoiding confrontation with a malicious boss. Avoid getting defensive or emotional, and focus on communicating your point of view in a calm and respectful manner.

Focus on Solutions

Rather than focusing on the problem or assigning blame, focus on finding a solution to the issue at hand. Offer suggestions or ideas for how to resolve the situation, and be open to compromise.

Use "I" Statements

When communicating with your boss, use "I" statements rather than "you" statements. For example, say "I feel frustrated when..."

rather than "You are making me angry by...". This can help you avoid sounding accusatory or confrontational.

Take a Break

If a conversation with your boss is becoming heated or confrontational, take a break to cool off. Excuse yourself from the conversation and come back when you are feeling more calm and composed.

Seek Mediation

If you are unable to resolve a conflict with your boss on your own, consider seeking mediation from a neutral third party. A mediator can help facilitate communication and find a solution that works for everyone involved.

Document Everything

In case of a confrontational situation, document everything. Keep a record of emails, conversations, and any incidents that occur. Having a record can help protect you if the situation escalates.

In conclusion, avoiding confrontation is an effective strategy for managing interactions with a malicious boss. By choosing your battles, staying professional, focusing on solutions, using "I" statements, taking a break, seeking mediation, and documenting everything, you can navigate difficult situations with your boss in a calm and constructive manner.

3. Building Trust and Rapport

Finding Common Ground

Building trust and rapport with a malicious boss can be challenging, but finding common ground can be a helpful strategy. Here are some tips for finding common ground with your boss:

1.1 Identify Shared Interests

Take some time to get to know your boss on a personal level. Find out what their hobbies, interests, and passions are. If you share similar interests, use that as a starting point for building a relationship.

1.2 Look for Shared Goals

If you and your boss are working towards the same goal, use that as a foundation for building trust and rapport. Work together to achieve the goal, and celebrate your successes along the way.

1.3 Find a Shared Vision

If you and your boss have different ideas about how to achieve a goal, try to find a shared vision that you can both agree on. This can help you work together more effectively and build trust in each other.

1.4 Ask for Feedback

Asking for feedback from your boss can be a powerful way to build trust and rapport. Listen to their feedback, take it into consideration, and use it to improve your performance.

1.5 Communicate Openly

Communicating openly and honestly with your boss can help build trust and rapport. Be transparent about your goals, concerns, and challenges, and encourage your boss to do the same.

1.6 Be Respectful

Respectful communication is key to building trust and rapport with a malicious boss. Avoid making negative comments or speaking negatively about your boss, and focus on finding constructive ways to communicate.

1.7 Show Empathy

Try to put yourself in your boss's shoes and understand their perspective. This can help you build empathy and trust with your boss, even if you don't always agree with their actions.

In conclusion, finding common ground with a malicious boss can be a helpful strategy for building trust and rapport. By identifying shared interests, looking for shared goals, finding a shared vision, asking for feedback, communicating openly, being respectful, and showing empathy, you can build a stronger relationship with your boss and work together more effectively.

Communicating Effectively

Communicating effectively with a malicious boss can be challenging, but it is a critical skill for managing your relationship with them. Here are some tips for effective communication:

1.1 Be Clear and Concise

When communicating with your boss, be clear and concise in your message. Avoid using jargon or technical terms that your boss may not understand, and focus on delivering your message in a straightforward and easy-to-understand manner.

1.2 Use Active Listening

Active listening is a key component of effective communication. Listen to your boss's words, tone, and body language, and respond in a way that shows you understand their message.

1.3 Be Empathetic

Empathy is the ability to understand and share the feelings of another person. Try to put yourself in your boss's shoes and understand their perspective. This can help you communicate more effectively and build trust with your boss.

1.4 Use Positive Language

Using positive language can help create a more positive and constructive atmosphere. Instead of focusing on problems, focus on solutions and use language that is supportive and encouraging.

1.5 Be Respectful

Respectful communication is critical when dealing with a malicious boss. Avoid making negative comments or speaking negatively about your boss, and focus on finding constructive ways to communicate.

1.6 Clarify Expectations

Clarifying expectations can help avoid misunderstandings and miscommunication. Be clear about what you expect from your boss and what they can expect from you.

1.7 Follow Up

Following up on conversations and agreements can help ensure that everyone is on the same page. Recap what was discussed, confirm next steps, and set a timeline for follow-up.

In conclusion, effective communication is critical when dealing with a malicious boss. By being clear and concise, using active listening, being empathetic, using positive language, being respectful, clarifying expectations, and following up, you can communicate more effectively with your boss and manage your relationship more effectively.

Managing Expectations

Managing expectations is a critical skill for dealing with a malicious boss. Here are some tips for managing expectations:

1.1 Clarify Expectations

Clarifying expectations is the first step in managing them. Take the time to discuss your boss's expectations and make sure you understand them. Be clear about what you can and cannot deliver, and be realistic about timelines and resources.

1.2 Set Realistic Goals

Setting realistic goals is important for managing expectations. Make sure the goals you set are achievable and measurable, and communicate them clearly to your boss.

1.3 Communicate Progress

Regularly communicating progress is an important part of managing expectations. Keep your boss updated on your progress, share successes and challenges, and ask for feedback.

1.4 Anticipate Problems

Anticipating problems before they occur can help you manage expectations more effectively. Consider potential obstacles and challenges, and have a plan in place to address them.

1.5 Manage Upward

Managing upward is the practice of effectively communicating with your boss to meet their expectations. Make sure you understand your boss's priorities and work to align your goals and actions with them.

1.6 Be Transparent

Transparency is key when managing expectations. Be honest about challenges, setbacks, and delays, and communicate openly with your boss about the steps you are taking to address them.

1.7 Seek Feedback

Seeking feedback is an important part of managing expectations. Ask your boss for feedback on your progress, and use it to improve your performance.

In conclusion, managing expectations is a critical skill for dealing with a malicious boss. By clarifying expectations, setting realistic goals, communicating progress, anticipating problems, managing upward, being transparent, and seeking feedback, you can manage expectations more effectively and build a stronger relationship with your boss.

4. Protecting Yourself

Documenting Everything

Dealing with a malicious boss can be a challenging experience, and it's important to take steps to protect yourself. One of the most important steps you can take is to document everything that happens in the workplace. Here are some tips for effective documentation:

1.1 Keep a Journal

Keeping a journal is a simple but effective way to document your interactions with your boss. Write down everything that happens, including conversations, emails, and other forms of communication. Be as detailed as possible, including dates, times, and the names of any witnesses.

1.2 Save Emails and Other Correspondence

Save all emails, memos, and other forms of correspondence with your boss. This can be important evidence if you need to make a complaint or take legal action.

1.3 Take Notes

Take notes during meetings with your boss, including any commitments made or decisions reached. If possible, send a follow-up email summarizing the key points of the meeting and asking your boss to confirm that your summary is accurate.

1.4 Keep a Record of Performance Reviews

Performance reviews can be an important part of your documentation. Keep a record of all performance reviews, including any comments or criticisms made by your boss. This can be useful if you need to challenge a negative review or if you believe your boss is unfairly targeting you.

1.5 Seek Witnesses

If possible, seek witnesses to any incidents or conversations with your boss. Ask them to provide a written statement or to testify on your behalf if necessary.

1.6 Don't Alter or Destroy Evidence

It's important to maintain the integrity of your documentation. Don't alter or destroy any evidence, and don't disclose it to anyone unless necessary.

1.7 Seek Legal Advice

If you believe that you have been the victim of discrimination or harassment by your boss, seek legal advice. An attorney can help you understand your rights and options and can advise you on how best to proceed.

In conclusion, documenting everything is an important step in protecting yourself when dealing with a malicious boss. By keeping a journal, saving emails and other correspondence, taking notes, keeping a record of performance reviews, seeking witnesses, maintaining the integrity of your documentation, and seeking legal advice if necessary, you can build a strong case and protect your rights.

Understanding Your Legal Rights

Dealing with a malicious boss can be a challenging experience, but it's important to know your legal rights. Here are some key legal rights that protect employees in the workplace:

1.1 Title VII of the Civil Rights Act of 1964

Title VII prohibits employment discrimination on the basis of race, color, religion, sex, or national origin. This means that it is illegal for your boss to discriminate against you on these grounds, including harassment and retaliation.

1.2 Americans with Disabilities Act (ADA)

The ADA prohibits discrimination against employees with disabilities. This includes providing reasonable accommodations to allow employees with disabilities to perform their jobs.

1.3 Age Discrimination in Employment Act (ADEA)

The ADEA prohibits discrimination against employees who are 40 years of age or older. This includes harassment and retaliation based on age.

1.4 Family and Medical Leave Act (FMLA)

The FMLA provides eligible employees with up to 12 weeks of unpaid leave per year for certain medical and family-related reasons. This includes caring for a newborn child, a seriously ill family member, or recovering from a serious medical condition.

1.5 Fair Labor Standards Act (FLSA)

The FLSA establishes minimum wage and overtime pay requirements for most employees in the United States. This means that your boss must pay you at least the minimum wage and overtime if you work more than 40 hours per week.

1.6 Occupational Safety and Health Act (OSHA)

OSHA sets safety and health standards in the workplace to protect employees from workplace hazards. This includes providing training, protective equipment, and safety measures to prevent injuries and illnesses.

1.7 National Labor Relations Act (NLRA)

The NLRA protects employees' rights to organize and engage in collective bargaining. This includes the right to form or join a union, to bargain collectively with your employer, and to engage in protected concerted activities with your coworkers.

In conclusion, understanding your legal rights is an important step in protecting yourself when dealing with a malicious boss. By knowing your rights under Title VII, the ADA, the ADEA, the FMLA, the FLSA, OSHA, and the NLRA, you can better protect yourself from discrimination, harassment, retaliation, and other workplace violations. If you believe your rights have been violated, seek legal advice from an attorney or a government agency that enforces employment laws.

Knowing When to Seek Help

Dealing with a malicious boss can be a stressful and challenging experience. You may feel isolated, helpless, and unsure of what to do. However, it's important to know that you don't have to face this situation alone. Here are some signs that it may be time to seek help:

1. Your Boss's Behavior Is Affecting Your Health

If your boss's behavior is causing you significant stress, anxiety, or depression, it may be affecting your physical and mental health. You may experience symptoms such as headaches, insomnia, fatigue, or a weakened immune system. If this is the case, it's important to seek help from a mental health professional, such as a therapist or counselor.

2. Your Boss Is Breaking the Law

If your boss is engaging in illegal behavior, such as discrimination, harassment, or retaliation, it's important to report it to the appropriate authorities. This may include filing a complaint with the Equal Employment Opportunity Commission (EEOC), the Occupational Safety and Health Administration (OSHA), or a state labor agency.

3. Your Boss Is Putting You in Physical Danger

If your boss is engaging in behavior that puts you in physical danger, such as verbal or physical abuse, it's important to seek help immediately. This may include contacting law enforcement or seeking a restraining order.

4. You Have Tried to Resolve the Issue on Your Own Without Success

If you have tried to address the issue with your boss directly, but the behavior continues, it may be time to seek help from a higher authority. This may include contacting HR, a supervisor, or an employment law attorney.

5. Your Coworkers Are Also Being Affected

If your boss's behavior is affecting other coworkers as well, it may be time to seek help as a group. This may include organizing a meeting with HR, a supervisor, or an employment law attorney to address the issue together.

In conclusion, dealing with a malicious boss can be a difficult experience, but it's important to know that you don't have to face it alone. If you are experiencing significant stress, your boss is breaking the law, you are in physical danger, you have tried to resolve the issue without success, or your coworkers are also being affected, it may be time to seek help from a mental health professional, a government agency, or an employment law attorney. Remember, your safety and well-being are the top priority, and there are resources available to help you.

5. Playing the Long Game

Strategic Planning for Your Career

Dealing with a malicious boss can be a challenging experience, but it's important to not lose sight of your long-term goals. One way to stay focused on your career aspirations is to engage in strategic planning. Here are some tips for playing the long game:

1. Define Your Career Goals

Take some time to think about what you want to achieve in your career. What are your long-term aspirations? What steps do you need to take to achieve those goals? Defining your career goals can help you stay focused and motivated, even in the face of challenges.

2. Identify Your Strengths and Weaknesses

Understanding your strengths and weaknesses can help you identify areas for improvement and develop a plan to address them. Consider taking a skills assessment or seeking feedback from coworkers or mentors.

3. Build Your Network

Building a strong professional network can be a valuable asset in your career. Attend industry events, connect with colleagues on LinkedIn, and seek out mentorship opportunities to expand your network.

4. Develop Your Skills

Investing in your professional development can help you stay competitive and prepare for future career opportunities. Consider taking courses, attending conferences, or seeking out on-the-job training opportunities to build your skills.

5. Seek Out Opportunities for Growth

Look for opportunities to take on new responsibilities or projects that will help you build your skills and demonstrate your value to your employer. Consider volunteering for cross-functional teams or seeking out leadership opportunities.

6. Stay Up-to-Date on Industry Trends

Staying informed about industry trends and developments can help you anticipate changes and stay ahead of the curve. Subscribe to industry publications, attend conferences, and participate in professional organizations to stay informed.

By engaging in strategic planning, you can stay focused on your long-term career goals and take proactive steps to achieve them. While dealing with a malicious boss can be challenging, don't let it derail your career aspirations. Remember, you are in control of your own professional development and can take steps to build a successful career, regardless of the challenges you face.

Finding Allies Within the Organization

Dealing with a malicious boss can be a challenging experience, but it's important to remember that you are not alone. Finding allies within the organization can help you navigate difficult situations, build support for your ideas, and advocate for yourself and your career goals. Here are some tips for finding allies within your organization:

1. Build Relationships with Coworkers

Building positive relationships with your coworkers can help you create a network of support within the organization. Take the time to get to know your colleagues, offer to help with projects or tasks, and show appreciation for their contributions.

2. Seek Out Mentors and Advocates

Finding mentors and advocates within the organization can help you navigate difficult situations and advocate for your career goals. Look for senior leaders or colleagues who can offer guidance and support, and be proactive in seeking out mentorship opportunities.

3. Join Employee Resource Groups

Employee resource groups (ERGs) are often established to support and advocate for employees from diverse backgrounds. Joining an ERG can help you build relationships with colleagues who share your interests and experiences, and can provide a platform to discuss common challenges.

4. Participate in Professional Development Opportunities

Participating in professional development opportunities, such as training programs, conferences, or workshops, can help you build relationships with colleagues from different departments or areas of the organization. These experiences can also provide opportunities to showcase your skills and expertise, which can help build support for your career goals.

5. Be Visible and Proactive

Being visible and proactive within the organization can help you build relationships and establish yourself as a valuable contributor. Look for opportunities to volunteer for committees or task forces, and be proactive in seeking out opportunities to collaborate with colleagues on projects or initiatives.

Finding allies within your organization can be a valuable asset in navigating challenging situations and building support for your career goals. By building positive relationships with your colleagues, seeking out mentorship opportunities, and being proactive in seeking out opportunities to contribute, you can establish yourself as a valued member of the organization and build a network of support to help you achieve your goals.

Creating Opportunities for Growth

Dealing with a malicious boss can make it challenging to find opportunities for growth and career advancement. However, it's important to remember that you are ultimately responsible for your own career development and should actively seek out opportunities to grow and develop. Here are some tips for creating opportunities for growth, even in the face of a difficult work environment:

1. Identify Your Strengths and Development Areas

Take the time to reflect on your strengths and areas for development. This can help you identify areas where you want to grow and develop, as well as opportunities to leverage your strengths in your current role or pursue new career paths.

2. Seek Out Learning Opportunities

Look for opportunities to learn and develop new skills, both within and outside of your current role. This might include taking on new projects or responsibilities, participating in training programs, attending conferences or workshops, or pursuing additional education or certification.

3. Network and Build Relationships

Networking and building relationships with colleagues, both within and outside of your organization, can help you discover new opportunities and gain insights into different career paths.

Attend industry events, join professional organizations, and seek out mentors or sponsors who can offer guidance and support.

4. Be Proactive in Seeking Out Opportunities

Don't wait for opportunities to come to you – be proactive in seeking out new experiences and challenges. This might involve volunteering for new projects or initiatives, seeking out leadership roles within your organization, or exploring new career paths.

5. Advocate for Yourself

Don't be afraid to speak up and advocate for yourself and your career goals. This might involve having conversations with your boss or other senior leaders about your career aspirations, or seeking out feedback and guidance from colleagues or mentors.

Dealing with a malicious boss can make it difficult to find opportunities for growth and career advancement. However, by identifying your strengths and development areas, seeking out learning opportunities, networking and building relationships, being proactive in seeking out opportunities, and advocating for yourself, you can create opportunities for growth and development even in the face of challenging circumstances. Remember that you are ultimately responsible for your own career development, and by taking an active approach to your career, you can achieve your goals and reach your full potential.

6. Dealing with Office Politics

Understanding the Power Dynamics

Office politics are an inevitable part of any workplace, and dealing with them can be challenging. Understanding the power dynamics at play can help you navigate office politics more effectively and minimize their impact on your work and career. Here are some tips for understanding power dynamics in the workplace:

1. Identify the Key Players

Take the time to observe the people and groups who hold the most power in your workplace. This might include senior leaders, influential employees, or informal networks of colleagues. Understanding who holds the power can help you navigate the office politics more effectively and identify potential allies and adversaries.

2. Understand the Sources of Power

There are many different sources of power in the workplace, including formal authority, expertise, relationships, and personal charisma. Understanding which sources of power are most valued in your workplace can help you understand how decisions are made and who holds the most influence.

3. Watch for Non-Verbal Cues

Pay attention to non-verbal cues such as body language, tone of voice, and facial expressions. These can often reveal underlying power dynamics that are not immediately apparent. For example, a senior leader may use a dismissive tone of voice when speaking to a junior employee, which can signal a power imbalance.

4. Build Relationships and Alliances

Building strong relationships with colleagues can help you navigate office politics more effectively. Seek out allies who share your goals and values, and work together to achieve common objectives. Be careful not to get drawn into toxic or negative alliances, however, as these can be damaging to your reputation and career.

5. Stay Focused on Your Goals

It's important to stay focused on your goals and priorities, even in the midst of office politics. Avoid getting drawn into petty arguments or power struggles, and focus on delivering high-quality work and achieving your objectives. This can help you build a reputation as a reliable and competent employee, which can ultimately be more important than any power struggle.

Dealing with office politics can be challenging, but by understanding the power dynamics at play, watching for non-verbal cues, building relationships and alliances, and staying focused on your goals, you can navigate these dynamics more effectively and minimize their impact on your work and career. Remember to approach office politics with a sense of professionalism and integrity, and to prioritize building positive relationships and delivering high-quality work above all else.

Navigating Cliques and Alliances

Cliques and alliances are a common feature of office politics. These informal networks of colleagues can be both beneficial and challenging to navigate, depending on how they are structured and the goals they pursue. Here are some tips for navigating cliques and alliances in the workplace:

1. Observe the Dynamics

The first step in navigating cliques and alliances is to observe their dynamics. Pay attention to who is in the group, how they interact with each other, and what they are working towards. This can give you a sense of the group's goals and how they might impact your work.

2. Avoid Taking Sides

While it can be tempting to align yourself with a particular group, it's important to avoid taking sides too early on. Instead, focus on building positive relationships with colleagues across the organization and avoid getting drawn into internal power struggles.

3. Build Your Own Network

Building your own network of allies and colleagues can help you navigate office politics more effectively. Seek out colleagues who share your values and goals, and work together to achieve common objectives. This can help you build a reputation as a reliable and competent employee, and provide a support system outside of any cliques or alliances.

4. Be Aware of Office Politics

It's important to stay aware of office politics, even if you're not directly involved in any cliques or alliances. Pay attention to any power struggles or conflicts that may be brewing, and be prepared to navigate these dynamics with professionalism and integrity.

5. Maintain a Professional Image

Finally, it's important to maintain a professional image in the workplace. Avoid gossiping or spreading rumors, and focus on delivering high-quality work and building positive relationships with colleagues across the organization. This can help you build a reputation as a respected and competent employee, and ensure that you are not negatively impacted by any office politics or internal power struggles.

In conclusion, navigating cliques and alliances in the workplace can be challenging, but by observing the dynamics, avoiding taking sides, building your own network, staying aware of office politics, and maintaining a professional image, you can navigate these dynamics more effectively and minimize their impact on your work and career. Remember to prioritize building positive relationships with colleagues, and to approach office politics with a sense of professionalism and integrity.

Avoiding Gossip and Rumors

Gossip and rumors can be damaging to both individuals and organizations. They can undermine trust, create a toxic work environment, and ultimately harm productivity and morale. Here are some strategies for avoiding gossip and rumors in the workplace:

1. Don't Engage in Gossip

The easiest way to avoid gossip is to simply not engage in it. Refuse to participate in conversations that are focused on negative rumors or speculation about colleagues. If someone tries to engage you in gossip, politely redirect the conversation to a more positive topic.

2. Be Careful What You Share

Be mindful of what you share with colleagues. Don't disclose sensitive or confidential information that could be used to fuel rumors or gossip. If you're not sure whether something is appropriate to share, err on the side of caution and keep it to yourself.

3. Check Your Sources

If you hear a rumor or gossip about a colleague, check your sources before taking it at face value. Ask yourself whether the information is credible and whether it comes from a reliable source. If you're not sure, it's better to assume that the information is unreliable and avoid spreading it further.

4. Address Gossip Directly

If you hear gossip or rumors about yourself or a colleague, address it directly with the person spreading the information. Be clear and assertive, but also calm and professional. Explain why the gossip is harmful and ask the person to stop spreading it.

5. Focus on the Positive

Instead of engaging in negative conversations or gossip, focus on the positive aspects of your work and colleagues. Share accomplishments and successes, and celebrate the achievements of your colleagues. This can help create a more positive work environment and reduce the likelihood of negative rumors and gossip.

6. Report Harassment or Discrimination

If you witness or experience gossip or rumors that are based on harassment or discrimination, it's important to report it to HR or a supervisor. This type of behavior is unacceptable and can have serious consequences for both the individuals involved and the organization as a whole.

In conclusion, avoiding gossip and rumors in the workplace is an important part of creating a positive and productive work environment. By refusing to engage in gossip, being careful with what you share, checking your sources, addressing gossip directly, focusing on the positive, and reporting harassment or discrimination, you can help create a workplace that is respectful, professional, and supportive. Remember, positive communication is key to a successful and thriving workplace culture.

7. Managing Conflicts

Resolving Disagreements

Conflict is a natural part of any workplace, but it's important to manage it effectively to maintain a positive work environment and productive relationships. Here are some strategies for resolving disagreements in the workplace:

1. Identify the Issue

The first step in resolving any disagreement is to identify the issue at hand. This means being clear about the specific problem or concern that is causing the conflict. Take the time to listen to all parties involved and get a clear understanding of their perspectives.

2. Focus on Interests, Not Positions

Often, disagreements arise because people are focused on their positions rather than their interests. Try to understand the underlying interests and needs of all parties involved, and look for solutions that address those interests. This can help shift the focus from winning or losing to finding a mutually beneficial solution.

3. Communicate Clearly and Respectfully

Effective communication is key to resolving conflicts. Be clear and direct when communicating your own needs and concerns, and listen actively to the perspectives of others. Avoid blaming or attacking language, and focus on finding common ground.

4. Explore Different Options

Once you have a clear understanding of the issue and interests involved, explore different options for resolving the conflict. Brainstorm possible solutions, and be open to creative ideas and compromises. Remember, the goal is to find a solution that works for everyone, not just one party.

5. Negotiate a Solution

Once you have explored different options, it's time to negotiate a solution. This means working together to find a mutually beneficial agreement that addresses the interests and needs of all parties involved. Be flexible and willing to compromise, and focus on finding a solution that everyone can live with.

6. Follow Up and Monitor Progress

Once a solution has been agreed upon, it's important to follow up and monitor progress. This means checking in regularly to ensure that everyone is following through on their commitments, and that the solution is working as intended. If issues arise, be willing to revisit the solution and make adjustments as needed.

In conclusion, resolving disagreements and managing conflicts in the workplace requires effective communication, a focus on interests rather than positions, and a willingness to explore different options and negotiate a mutually beneficial solution. By following these strategies, you can help maintain a positive work environment and productive relationships with your colleagues.

Negotiating Win-Win Solutions

Negotiating win-win solutions is a powerful way to resolve conflicts and reach mutually beneficial agreements. Here are some strategies for negotiating win-win solutions in the workplace:

1. Understand the Interests and Needs of All Parties Involved

To negotiate a win-win solution, it's important to understand the interests and needs of all parties involved. This means taking the time to listen to everyone's perspectives and concerns, and identifying the underlying interests and motivations that are driving their positions.

2. Look for Shared Interests and Goals

Once you understand the interests and needs of all parties involved, look for shared interests and goals. These are the areas where there is potential for mutual benefit and collaboration. By focusing on shared interests, you can create a foundation for a win-win solution.

3. Brainstorm Creative Solutions

Once you have identified shared interests and goals, it's time to brainstorm creative solutions. Be open to new ideas and perspectives, and look for solutions that meet the needs and interests of all parties involved. Don't be afraid to think outside the box and consider unconventional solutions.

4. Evaluate the Pros and Cons of Each Option

Once you have generated a list of potential solutions, evaluate the pros and cons of each option. Consider factors such as feasibility, impact on different parties, and long-term implications. Look for solutions that offer the most benefits while minimizing negative impacts.

5. Work Together to Refine the Solution

Once you have identified the most promising solution, work together to refine and finalize the details. This may involve making adjustments or compromises to ensure that the solution is acceptable to all parties involved. Be willing to listen and make changes as needed to achieve a mutually beneficial outcome.

6. Communicate Clearly and Follow Through on Commitments

Once a win-win solution has been reached, it's important to communicate clearly and follow through on commitments. Make sure that everyone understands their roles and responsibilities, and that expectations are clearly defined. Check in regularly to ensure that everyone is following through on their commitments and that the solution is working as intended.

In conclusion, negotiating win-win solutions requires a focus on understanding the interests and needs of all parties involved, identifying shared interests and goals, brainstorming creative solutions, evaluating options, refining the solution, and following through on commitments. By following these strategies, you can build positive relationships and achieve mutually beneficial outcomes in the workplace.

Mediating Disputes

Mediating disputes is an important skill for anyone working in a team or managing others. Mediation involves facilitating communication and negotiation between two or more parties in conflict, with the goal of finding a mutually acceptable solution. Here are some strategies for effective mediation:

1. Remain Neutral and Impartial

As a mediator, it's important to remain neutral and impartial. This means avoiding taking sides or showing favoritism, and focusing on the interests and needs of both parties involved in the dispute. Stay objective and avoid expressing personal opinions or judgments.

2. Listen Carefully to Both Sides

Effective mediation requires active listening. Listen carefully to both sides of the dispute, and encourage them to share their perspectives and concerns. Ask open-ended questions to clarify their positions and interests, and rephrase their statements to ensure that you understand their points of view.

3. Identify Common Ground and Shared Interests

Look for areas of common ground and shared interests between the parties involved in the dispute. This can provide a basis for finding a mutually acceptable solution. Focus on the underlying needs and interests of both parties, rather than their positions or demands.

4. Generate Options for Resolution

Brainstorm options for resolving the dispute that meet the needs and interests of both parties. Encourage creative thinking and consider a range of possible solutions. Remember that the goal is to find a mutually acceptable solution that meets the underlying needs and interests of both parties.

5. Help Parties Evaluate Options and Reach a Decision

Once a range of options has been generated, help the parties evaluate the pros and cons of each option and reach a decision. Encourage them to consider the long-term implications of their decisions and how they will affect their ongoing relationship. Facilitate the negotiation process to help them reach a mutually acceptable agreement.

6. Follow Up to Ensure Agreement is Implemented

After an agreement has been reached, it's important to follow up to ensure that it is implemented. Check in with both parties to ensure that they are following through on their commitments and that the agreement is working as intended. If issues arise, be prepared to facilitate further communication and negotiation.

In conclusion, effective mediation involves remaining neutral and impartial, listening carefully to both sides, identifying common ground and shared interests, generating options for resolution, helping parties evaluate options and reach a decision, and following up to ensure that the agreement is implemented. By developing these skills, you can help to resolve disputes and build positive relationships in the workplace.

8. Addressing Underperformance

Providing Constructive Feedback

Addressing underperformance is an important part of managing a team, but it can be a difficult conversation to have. One key strategy for addressing underperformance is to provide constructive feedback. Here are some tips for providing effective feedback:

1. Be Specific and Concrete

When providing feedback, be specific and concrete. Avoid generalizations and provide examples of specific behaviors or actions that need improvement. This can help the employee understand what they need to do differently and how they can improve.

2. Focus on Behaviors, not Personal Characteristics

When providing feedback, focus on the employee's behaviors and actions, rather than their personal characteristics. This can help avoid personal attacks or defensiveness. Instead of saying "you're lazy," focus on specific behaviors, such as "you missed three deadlines last week."

3. Use the "Sandwich" Technique

The "sandwich" technique is a popular method for providing feedback. It involves sandwiching constructive feedback between positive feedback. Start with positive feedback, then provide constructive feedback, and end with positive feedback. For example, "I really appreciate the effort you put into this project, but I think we need to work on meeting deadlines more consistently. That being said, I know you have the skills to improve and I'm confident we can make progress together."

4. Ask for the Employee's Input

When providing feedback, ask the employee for their input and perspective. This can help them feel heard and valued, and can also help you understand their perspective. Ask open-ended questions, such as "What do you think went well with the project? What could have been done differently?"

5. Set Clear Goals and Expectations

After providing feedback, set clear goals and expectations for improvement. Be specific about what you want the employee to do differently and by when. Make sure the goals are achievable and measurable, so progress can be tracked over time.

6. Follow Up Regularly

After providing feedback and setting goals, follow up regularly to check on progress and provide ongoing support and guidance. Celebrate successes and offer additional feedback as needed. This can help the employee stay motivated and on track towards improvement.

In conclusion, addressing underperformance is an important part of managing a team, and providing constructive feedback is a key strategy for addressing it. By being specific and concrete, focusing on behaviors, using the "sandwich" technique, asking for the employee's input, setting clear goals and expectations, and following up regularly, you can provide effective feedback and help employees improve their performance.

Coaching and Mentoring

Coaching and Mentoring

Coaching and mentoring are two similar but distinct approaches to professional development. Both involve providing guidance, feedback, and support to help individuals reach their full potential. However, there are some key differences between the two. Coaching is typically focused on improving performance in a specific area, while mentoring is more focused on broader career development. In this chapter, we will explore the benefits of coaching and mentoring, and provide guidance on how to be an effective coach or mentor.

Benefits of Coaching and Mentoring

Coaching and mentoring have a number of benefits for both the individual being coached or mentored, as well as the organization as a whole. Some of the key benefits include:

1. Improved Performance: Coaching and mentoring can help individuals identify areas for improvement and develop new skills and strategies to achieve their goals. This can lead to improved performance, both in terms of productivity and quality of work.

2. Increased Engagement: When individuals feel supported and encouraged in their professional development, they are more

likely to be engaged and invested in their work. Coaching and mentoring can help individuals feel more connected to their work and their organization.

3. Career Development: Mentoring, in particular, can be a valuable tool for career development. Mentors can provide guidance on career paths, help individuals identify their strengths and weaknesses, and provide insights into the skills and experience needed to advance in their field.

4. Knowledge Sharing: Coaching and mentoring can help individuals learn from others with more experience and expertise. Mentors and coaches can share their knowledge, skills, and insights, helping others to develop their own skills and expertise.

5. Improved Retention: When individuals feel supported and valued by their organization, they are more likely to stay in their role and remain committed to the organization's goals.

Effective Coaching

Coaching can be a valuable tool for improving performance and developing new skills. However, it is important to approach coaching in the right way to ensure that it is effective. Here are some tips for effective coaching:

1. Set Clear Goals: It is important to establish clear goals and expectations for the coaching relationship. This will help both the coach and the individual being coached to stay focused and make progress toward specific objectives.

2. Provide Feedback: Feedback is an important part of the coaching process. It is important to provide feedback in a constructive and supportive way, highlighting areas for improvement and providing specific suggestions for how to improve.

3. Be Supportive: Coaching is a supportive process, and it is important to be encouraging and positive throughout. This can help the individual being coached feel more confident and motivated to improve.

4. Use Active Listening: Active listening is an important skill for coaches. It involves listening carefully to what the individual is saying, asking clarifying questions, and reflecting back what has been said to ensure understanding.

5. Focus on Solutions: Coaching should be focused on finding solutions to problems or challenges. This involves helping the individual being coached identify potential solutions and strategies to overcome obstacles.

Effective Mentoring

Mentoring is a broader approach to professional development, focused on career growth and advancement. Here are some tips for effective mentoring:

1. Build a Relationship: Mentoring is built on a relationship of trust and respect. It is important to take the time to get to know the individual being mentored and understand their goals and aspirations.

2. Share Your Expertise: Mentors have a wealth of knowledge and experience to share with their mentees. It is important to be open and generous with your knowledge, and to provide guidance and support in areas where the mentee may be struggling.

3. Challenge and Encourage: Mentoring should involve both challenge and encouragement. It is important to push the mentee to reach their full potential, while also providing support and encouragement along the way.

4. Providing feedback is a crucial part of managing underperformance, and it is an essential skill for any manager or leader to possess. However, providing constructive feedback can be challenging, especially when dealing with sensitive topics or difficult individuals. One effective way to provide feedback is through coaching.

Coaching is a process of developing an individual's skills and abilities through guidance and support. It is a collaborative and empowering approach that encourages individuals to take ownership of their development and progress towards their goals. The coaching approach to feedback focuses on building self-awareness, identifying strengths and areas for improvement, and setting goals for improvement. In this way, coaching can help individuals to develop their skills and improve their performance over time.

To provide effective feedback using a coaching approach, there are several key principles to keep in mind:

1. Create a Safe and Supportive Environment: It is essential to create a safe and supportive environment that encourages open communication and constructive feedback. This means setting aside time to meet with the individual in a private and comfortable setting, actively listening to their concerns and feedback, and avoiding judgment or criticism.

2. Be Specific and Objective: When providing feedback, it is important to be specific and objective. Focus on the individual's behavior and actions, not their personality or character. Use concrete examples and provide specific feedback on what the individual is doing well and where they can improve.

3. Focus on Development: The coaching approach to feedback focuses on development rather than criticism. This means setting clear goals and objectives for improvement, providing ongoing support and guidance, and celebrating progress along the way.

4. Encourage Self-Reflection: Encouraging self-reflection is an essential part of the coaching process. This means encouraging the individual to reflect on their strengths and weaknesses, to identify areas for improvement, and to develop strategies to address these areas.

5. Provide Ongoing Support: Coaching is an ongoing process, and providing ongoing support is essential to ensure long-term success. This means checking in regularly with the individual, providing ongoing feedback and guidance, and adjusting goals and objectives as needed.

Using the coaching approach to feedback can be a powerful tool for managing underperformance. By creating a safe and supportive environment, being specific and objective, focusing on development, encouraging self-reflection, and providing ongoing support, managers and leaders can help individuals to develop their skills and improve their performance over time. In this way, coaching can be a valuable tool for building a high-performing team and achieving organizational goals.

Mentoring is a long-term development strategy that involves a senior or more experienced employee sharing their knowledge and experience with a less experienced employee. The goal of mentoring is to help the mentee develop new skills, learn from the mentor's experiences, and build a professional network. Mentoring can be an invaluable resource for employees at any stage in their careers, but it can be especially useful for those just starting out or seeking to advance to the next level.

There are two primary types of mentoring: formal and informal. Formal mentoring is typically structured by the organization, with a designated mentor and mentee. Informal mentoring, on the other hand, is more organic and typically arises from a relationship that develops naturally between two colleagues. Both types of mentoring can be effective, depending on the needs and preferences of the individuals involved.

Effective mentoring requires both the mentor and mentee to be committed to the relationship. The mentor should be willing to invest their time and energy in the mentee, providing guidance and support along the way. The mentee, in turn, should be open to feedback, receptive to new ideas, and willing to take action on the advice and guidance provided by the mentor.

One of the key benefits of mentoring is the opportunity for the mentee to learn from the mentor's experiences. Mentors can provide valuable insights into the industry, the organization, and the skills and behaviors necessary for success. Mentees can benefit from the mentor's perspective and advice, as well as the mentor's network of contacts and resources.

Another benefit of mentoring is the opportunity for the mentee to develop new skills and competencies. The mentor can provide guidance on specific tasks or projects, as well as on broader skills such as leadership, communication, and strategic thinking. The mentor can also provide feedback on the mentee's progress and help identify areas for improvement.

Mentoring can also be a valuable tool for career development. Mentors can help mentees navigate the organizational landscape, identify potential career paths, and develop a plan for achieving their career goals. Mentors can also provide introductions and recommendations to other professionals and help mentees build their professional network.

To be effective, mentoring should be a two-way street. While the mentor is providing guidance and support, the mentee should also be contributing to the relationship. Mentees can ask thoughtful questions, seek out feedback, and be open to learning from the mentor's experiences. They can also share their own perspectives and insights, which can be valuable to the mentor.

In addition to the benefits of mentoring for the individual, mentoring can also have positive impacts on the organization as a whole. By developing a culture of mentoring, organizations can foster collaboration, knowledge sharing, and talent development. Mentoring can also help build a more diverse and inclusive workforce, by providing opportunities for underrepresented groups to connect with more experienced professionals and gain access to new opportunities.

In conclusion, mentoring is a powerful tool for professional development and career advancement. By connecting less experienced employees with more experienced mentors, organizations can help build a culture of learning and development, foster collaboration and knowledge sharing, and support the growth and development of their workforce. Effective mentoring requires a commitment from both the mentor and mentee, but the benefits can be significant for both the individual and the organization.

Developing Performance Improvement Plans

A performance improvement plan (PIP) is a tool used by managers to help underperforming employees improve their performance. It is a structured approach to identify areas where the employee is struggling and create a plan for improvement. The goal of a PIP is to provide support and resources to the employee to help them succeed in their role. In this chapter, we will discuss the process of creating a PIP and how to effectively use it to improve employee performance.

Identify the Problem Areas:

The first step in creating a PIP is to identify the areas where the employee is struggling. This could be related to job tasks, communication, teamwork, or any other relevant areas. To do this, the manager should conduct a performance review and identify specific examples of where the employee is not meeting expectations. It is important to be specific and provide clear examples to the employee.

Set Goals and Objectives:

Once the problem areas have been identified, the manager should work with the employee to set goals and objectives for improvement. These goals should be specific, measurable, and achievable within a reasonable timeframe. It is important to involve the employee in setting these goals to ensure they are committed to achieving them.

Provide Resources and Support:

To help the employee achieve their goals, the manager should provide resources and support. This could include additional training, mentoring, coaching, or access to other resources. It is important to work with the employee to identify what resources they need to be successful.

Monitor Progress:

It is important to monitor the employee's progress regularly and provide feedback along the way. This will help the employee stay on track and make any necessary adjustments to their plan. The manager should schedule regular check-ins to review progress and provide feedback.

Document Everything:

It is important to document everything related to the PIP process. This includes the goals and objectives, resources provided, progress made, and any feedback provided. This documentation can be used to track the employee's progress, evaluate the effectiveness of the PIP, and ensure compliance with any legal requirements.

Communicate Clearly:

Throughout the PIP process, it is important to communicate clearly with the employee. This includes setting expectations, providing feedback, and addressing any concerns or issues that arise. The manager should be clear and concise in their communication to ensure the employee understands what is expected of them.

Address Any Barriers to Success:

If the employee is struggling to meet their goals, it is important to identify any barriers to success. This could be related to resources, training, workload, or any other factors that are impacting their performance. The manager should work with the employee to address these barriers and provide any necessary support.

Evaluate the Effectiveness of the PIP:

At the end of the PIP process, it is important to evaluate its effectiveness. This includes reviewing the progress made by the employee and determining whether they have met their goals. The manager should also evaluate the effectiveness of the PIP process itself and identify any areas for improvement.

In conclusion, a performance improvement plan is a powerful tool for managers to help underperforming employees improve their performance. By identifying problem areas, setting goals, providing resources and support, monitoring progress, documenting everything, communicating clearly, addressing barriers to success, and evaluating effectiveness, managers can help employees achieve their full potential and contribute to the success of the organization.

9. Overcoming Challenges

Dealing with Change and Uncertainty

Dealing with change and uncertainty is a challenge that most of us face at some point in our lives. It can be unsettling and can make us feel anxious and stressed. This challenge is particularly acute in the workplace, where change is often a constant. In this chapter, we will explore how to overcome these challenges and develop the resilience and adaptability needed to thrive in a changing environment.

Understanding Change and Uncertainty

Change and uncertainty can take many different forms in the workplace. It might involve a new boss, a shift in company strategy, or a major restructuring. It might also involve changes in the industry, such as new technologies or shifting market dynamics. Whatever the form it takes, change and uncertainty can have a significant impact on our work and our wellbeing.

One of the key challenges of dealing with change and uncertainty is that it can be difficult to predict the future. This can make it challenging to plan ahead and can create feelings of anxiety and fear. It's important to remember that change is a natural part of life, and that we have the ability to adapt and grow in response to it.

Developing Resilience

Resilience is the ability to bounce back from adversity and to maintain a positive outlook in the face of challenges. Developing resilience is key to dealing with change and uncertainty in the workplace. Here are some strategies for developing resilience:

1. Cultivate a Growth Mindset

A growth mindset is the belief that we can learn and grow through experience. This mindset can help us to see challenges as opportunities for growth, rather than as threats to our wellbeing. When faced with change and uncertainty, try to adopt a growth mindset and focus on what you can learn from the experience.

2. Build a Support Network

Having a strong support network can help us to weather the storms of change and uncertainty. This might include colleagues, friends, family members, or a mentor. Make sure to reach out to your support network when you need help or guidance.

3. Take Care of Yourself

Self-care is essential for maintaining resilience in the face of change and uncertainty. Make sure to take care of yourself physically, emotionally, and mentally. This might include getting enough sleep, eating well, exercising regularly, and engaging in activities that bring you joy.

4. Practice Mindfulness

Mindfulness is the practice of being present in the moment and observing our thoughts and feelings without judgment. This can help us to stay grounded and calm in the face of change and uncertainty. Consider incorporating mindfulness practices into your daily routine, such as meditation or deep breathing exercises.

Adapting to Change

Adapting to change involves learning new skills, adjusting to new environments, and embracing new perspectives. Here are some strategies for adapting to change:

1. Stay Positive

Maintaining a positive outlook can help us to stay motivated and engaged in the face of change. Try to focus on the opportunities that change presents, rather than on the challenges.

2. Be Open to Learning

Learning new skills and perspectives is key to adapting to change. Be open to new ideas and approaches, and be willing to learn from others.

3. Stay Flexible

Flexibility is essential for adapting to change. Be willing to try new things and to take on new challenges, even if they are outside of your comfort zone.

4. Communicate Effectively

Effective communication is key to adapting to change. Make sure to communicate your needs, concerns, and ideas clearly and respectfully.

Navigating Uncertainty

Navigating uncertainty can be challenging, as it can bring about a range of emotions and unexpected situations. However, it is a necessary skill to develop in today's fast-paced and ever-changing work environment. Here are some additional strategies for navigating uncertainty:

1. Embrace the Unknown: It's natural to want to avoid the unknown, but it's important to remember that it's impossible to predict the future with certainty. Instead of fearing the unknown, try to embrace it and see it as an opportunity to learn and grow. By doing this, you'll become more comfortable with the unexpected and be better equipped to handle it when it arises.

2. Stay Positive: During times of uncertainty, it's easy to become negative and focus on the worst-case scenarios. However, staying positive and focusing on the opportunities that uncertainty can bring can help you stay motivated and productive. Look for the silver lining and try to view uncertainty as a chance to explore new possibilities.

3. Be Adaptable: Being adaptable means being able to adjust to changing situations quickly. This is an essential skill to have when dealing with uncertainty. To be more adaptable, try to be open to new ideas and approaches, and be willing to adjust your plans as needed. This will help you stay flexible and responsive to changing circumstances.

4. Communicate Effectively: Good communication is essential during times of uncertainty. Make sure to keep your boss and colleagues informed about any changes or challenges you are facing. This will help you build trust and ensure that everyone is on the same page. It's also important to be a good listener and seek out feedback from others.

5. Stay Organized: When dealing with uncertainty, it can be helpful to stay organized. Keep track of important deadlines, appointments, and tasks, and make sure to prioritize your work based on what's most important. This will help you stay focused and avoid getting overwhelmed by all the uncertainties.

6. Take Care of Yourself: It's important to take care of yourself during times of uncertainty. Make sure to get enough sleep, eat well, and exercise regularly. This will help you stay healthy, happy, and resilient, even in the face of uncertainty.

7. Seek Support: Finally, don't be afraid to seek support when dealing with uncertainty. Talk to friends, family, or colleagues who can offer guidance and support. You may also want to consider working with a coach or mentor who can help you navigate the challenges of uncertainty and build your skills for the future.

By embracing the unknown, staying positive, being adaptable, communicating effectively, staying organized, taking care of yourself, and seeking support, you can successfully navigate uncertainty and come out stronger on the other side.

Managing Stress and Burnout

Managing stress and burnout is a crucial skill for anyone in a high-pressure work environment, especially when dealing with a malicious boss. Stress and burnout can have serious negative effects on your health, well-being, and job performance, so it's essential to learn how to manage them effectively. In this chapter, we'll explore some strategies for managing stress and burnout.

1. Recognize the signs of stress and burnout

The first step in managing stress and burnout is recognizing the signs. Some common symptoms of stress and burnout include:

- Feeling exhausted, both physically and emotionally

- Losing interest in work or other activities you used to enjoy

- Feeling cynical or pessimistic about work

- Having trouble sleeping or staying focused

- Getting sick more often than usual

If you're experiencing these symptoms, it's essential to take action to manage your stress and avoid burnout.

2. Create a self-care plan

Self-care is an essential aspect of managing stress and burnout. It's essential to take care of yourself physically, emotionally, and mentally. Some strategies for self-care include:

- Eating a healthy diet

- Exercising regularly

- Getting enough sleep

- Practicing relaxation techniques such as meditation or yoga

- Taking breaks throughout the workday

It's important to prioritize self-care and make it a part of your routine.

3. Set boundaries

Setting boundaries is another essential strategy for managing stress and burnout. It's important to set clear limits on your work hours, workload, and expectations. Some ways to set boundaries include:

- Saying no to additional tasks or responsibilities that you don't have time for

- Setting realistic deadlines and goals

- Limiting the amount of time you spend checking emails or taking work calls outside of work hours

Setting boundaries can help you manage your workload and prevent burnout.

4. Practice stress management techniques

There are many stress management techniques that you can practice to manage your stress levels. Some examples include:

- Deep breathing exercises

- Progressive muscle relaxation

- Visualization techniques

- Mindfulness meditation

It's essential to find stress management techniques that work for you and incorporate them into your daily routine.

5. Seek support

If you're struggling with stress and burnout, it's essential to seek support. Talk to trusted friends, family members, or coworkers about your struggles. Consider seeking professional help, such as therapy or counseling.

6. Take time off

Sometimes, the best way to manage stress and prevent burnout is to take a break. Taking time off from work can give you the chance to recharge, refocus, and come back to work feeling refreshed and energized. Consider taking a vacation, a mental health day, or a personal day.

In conclusion, managing stress and burnout is essential for anyone in a high-pressure work environment. By recognizing the signs of stress and burnout, creating a self-care plan, setting boundaries, practicing stress management techniques, seeking support, and taking time off, you can effectively manage your stress levels and prevent burnout. Remember to prioritize your well-being and take care of yourself.

Maintaining a Positive Attitude

Maintaining a positive attitude can be a challenge, especially when working in a difficult environment. However, it is essential for success, happiness, and overall well-being. A positive attitude can help you approach challenges with a clear mind, stay motivated, and build resilience in the face of adversity. In this chapter, we will explore some strategies for maintaining a positive attitude, even in the most challenging circumstances.

1. Focus on the Positive:

It is easy to get bogged down in negative thoughts and feelings, especially when dealing with a malicious boss. However, it is essential to focus on the positive aspects of your job, your life, and yourself. This can be challenging, but it is possible. Start by making a list of all the things that are going well in your life, no matter how small. This can include things like your health, your relationships, your home, and your hobbies. By focusing on the positive aspects of your life, you can shift your mindset and develop a more positive outlook.

2. Practice Gratitude:

Gratitude is a powerful tool for maintaining a positive attitude. When you focus on the things you are grateful for, you can shift your focus away from negative thoughts and emotions. Start by taking a few minutes each day to think about the things you are grateful for, such as your health, your job, your friends, and your family. You can also keep a gratitude journal, where you write down the things you are grateful for each day.

3. Practice Mindfulness:

Mindfulness is the practice of being present and fully engaged in the moment. It can help you develop a more positive attitude by helping you focus on the present moment, rather than dwelling on the past or worrying about the future. There are many ways to practice mindfulness, including meditation, yoga, and deep breathing exercises.

4. Surround Yourself with Positivity:

The people you surround yourself with can have a significant impact on your attitude and outlook on life. Try to surround yourself with positive, supportive people who lift you up and encourage you to be your best self. This can include friends, family, and colleagues who share your values and beliefs.

5. Take Care of Yourself:

Self-care is essential for maintaining a positive attitude. This includes taking care of your physical, emotional, and mental health. Make sure you are getting enough sleep, eating a healthy diet, and exercising regularly. You can also practice self-care by doing things you enjoy, such as reading, listening to music, or taking a long bath.

6. Find Meaning and Purpose:

Having a sense of purpose and meaning in your life can help you develop a more positive attitude. This can be challenging when working in a difficult environment, but it is possible. Try to find meaning in your work by focusing on the impact you are making, no matter how small. You can also find meaning and purpose in your hobbies, volunteer work, or other activities outside of work.

7. Embrace Challenges:

Challenges are a part of life, and they can help you grow and develop. Instead of seeing challenges as obstacles, try to embrace them as opportunities for growth and learning. This can help you develop a more positive attitude and build resilience in the face of adversity.

In conclusion, maintaining a positive attitude is essential for success, happiness, and overall well-being, especially when working in a difficult environment. By focusing on the positive, practicing gratitude, mindfulness, surrounding yourself with positivity, taking care of yourself, finding meaning and purpose, and embracing challenges, you can develop a more positive outlook on life and build resilience in the face of adversity.

10. Moving On

Knowing When It's Time to Leave

Moving on: Knowing When It's Time to Leave

It is a difficult decision to make but sometimes leaving your job is the best option. If you have tried all the strategies to cope with a malicious boss and you still find yourself in a toxic work environment, leaving might be the best solution. But how do you know when it's time to leave? This chapter will explore some of the signs that indicate it's time to move on and some steps you can take to make a smooth transition.

Signs That It's Time to Leave

1. Your health is suffering

A toxic work environment can take a toll on your mental and physical health. If you are experiencing symptoms such as chronic fatigue, anxiety, depression, headaches, or high blood pressure, it may be time to consider leaving your job.

2. You dread going to work

If the thought of going to work fills you with dread and anxiety, it may be a sign that you are no longer happy or fulfilled in your job.

This feeling of dread could be caused by a difficult boss, a toxic work environment, or a lack of motivation.

3. You have no room for growth

If you feel stuck in your job and there are no opportunities for growth or advancement, it may be time to consider leaving. Stagnation can lead to dissatisfaction and ultimately burnout.

4. You are not being compensated fairly

If you feel undervalued and underpaid for your work, it may be time to consider leaving. You deserve to be compensated fairly for your time, skills, and expertise.

5. You are not aligned with the company's values

If you find that you are not aligned with the company's values, mission, or culture, it may be difficult to find fulfillment and purpose in your work. This misalignment could lead to dissatisfaction and a lack of motivation.

Steps to Take When Leaving Your Job

1. Have a plan

Before you hand in your resignation, make sure you have a plan in place. Consider your financial situation, job prospects, and timeline for finding a new job. It's important to have a clear idea of what you want to do next and how you plan to get there.

2. Give notice

It's important to give your employer adequate notice when resigning. This will give your employer time to find a replacement and make necessary arrangements for your departure.

3. Be professional

Even if you are leaving due to a difficult boss or a toxic work environment, it's important to be professional and courteous in your resignation. Avoid burning bridges and maintain a positive relationship with your employer and colleagues.

4. Focus on the future

Instead of dwelling on the past, focus on the future and the opportunities that lie ahead. Use your experiences and skills to find a job that aligns with your values and goals.

5. Take care of yourself

Leaving a job can be a stressful and emotional experience. Make sure to take care of yourself during this transition. Seek support from friends, family, or a therapist if needed. Take time to rest, recharge, and reflect on your goals and aspirations.

Conclusion

Leaving a job can be a difficult decision, but sometimes it's necessary for your mental and physical health, career growth, and overall happiness. Recognizing the signs that it's time to move on and having a plan in place can make the transition smoother and less stressful. Remember to focus on the future, take care of yourself, and maintain a positive attitude.

Finding a New Job or Career Path

When dealing with a malicious boss, it is important to consider finding a new job or career path as a way to move on from the situation. While leaving a job may not always be the easiest or most convenient option, it can ultimately lead to a healthier and more fulfilling work environment. This chapter will explore the steps involved in finding a new job or career path.

1. Assessing Your Current Situation:

Before embarking on a job search, it is important to assess your current situation. Reflect on why you want to leave your current job and what you hope to gain from a new one. Take inventory of your skills, strengths, and values, and determine what kind of job or career path would align with them. This will help you to narrow down your search and focus on opportunities that are the best fit for you.

2. Updating Your Resume and Cover Letter:

Once you have a clear idea of what you are looking for, it is important to update your resume and cover letter. Highlight your skills and experiences that are most relevant to the job or career path you are pursuing. Consider tailoring your resume and cover letter for each job you apply for, as this can increase your chances of getting noticed by potential employers.

3. Networking:

Networking is an important part of any job search. Reach out to your contacts, including friends, family, former colleagues, and acquaintances, to let them know you are looking for a new job. Attend networking events, join professional organizations, and use social media to connect with professionals in your desired field. Building relationships with people who can vouch for your skills and experience can help you to find job opportunities that may not be advertised publicly.

4. Searching for Job Opportunities:

There are several ways to search for job opportunities. You can search online job boards and company websites, attend job fairs, and work with a recruiter or staffing agency. Consider using multiple methods to increase your chances of finding the right job for you.

5. Preparing for Interviews:

Once you have applied for a job, you may be invited to an interview. It is important to prepare for the interview by researching the company and the job, practicing common interview questions, and preparing examples of how your skills and experience align with the job requirements. Dress professionally, arrive early, and bring copies of your resume and cover letter to the interview.

6. Negotiating an Offer:

If you are offered a job, take time to evaluate the offer before accepting it. Consider factors such as salary, benefits, work-life balance, and opportunities for growth and development. If you are not satisfied with the initial offer, consider negotiating for better terms.

7. Resigning Gracefully:

If you decide to accept a new job, it is important to resign from your current job gracefully. Schedule a meeting with your boss to let them know you are leaving, provide ample notice, and offer to help with the transition. Thank your colleagues for their support and the opportunities they provided you.

In conclusion, finding a new job or career path can be a challenging process, but it can ultimately lead to a healthier and more fulfilling work environment. By assessing your current situation, updating your resume and cover letter, networking, searching for job opportunities, preparing for interviews, negotiating an offer, and resigning gracefully, you can successfully navigate the job search process and find a job that aligns with your skills, strengths, and values.

Building Resilience and Learning from Your Experience.

Building Resilience and Learning from Your Experience

Dealing with a malicious boss can be a challenging and stressful experience. It can take a toll on your emotional and mental health, as well as your professional and personal life. However, it is essential to learn from this experience and develop resilience to overcome future challenges.

Building resilience is the ability to adapt and bounce back from adversity. It is an essential skill to develop when dealing with a malicious boss, as it can help you stay motivated and positive. Here are some tips to help you build resilience and learn from your experience:

1. Reflect on your experience

Take some time to reflect on your experience with your malicious boss. Think about what worked and what didn't work, what you learned, and what you could have done differently. Be honest with yourself and avoid blaming yourself or others. Use this reflection to identify your strengths and weaknesses and create a plan to improve.

2. Develop a growth mindset

A growth mindset is the belief that you can learn and develop your abilities through hard work and dedication. It is essential to have a growth mindset when dealing with a malicious boss as it can help you stay positive and focused. Instead of seeing failure as a setback, see it as an opportunity to learn and grow.

3. Practice self-care

Self-care is essential to maintain your physical, emotional, and mental health. It can include activities such as exercise, meditation, spending time with loved ones, or pursuing a hobby. Make self-care a priority and set aside time for it regularly.

4. Seek support

Support from friends, family, or a therapist can help you cope with the stress of dealing with a malicious boss. Talk to someone you trust and share your experience. You can also join support groups or online forums to connect with others who have gone through similar experiences.

5. Develop coping skills

Developing coping skills can help you manage stress and anxiety. Coping skills can include deep breathing, visualization, positive self-talk, or problem-solving. Identify coping skills that work for you and practice them regularly.

6. Set goals

Setting goals can help you stay focused and motivated. Identify short-term and long-term goals and create a plan to achieve them. Focus on what you can control and avoid getting discouraged by setbacks.

7. Learn new skills

Learning new skills can help you build confidence and increase your value in the job market. Identify skills that you want to develop and pursue training or education opportunities.

8. Take action

Take action towards your goals and aspirations. Use the lessons you learned from your experience to make positive changes in your life and career. Don't be afraid to take risks and try new things.

Dealing with a malicious boss can be a challenging experience, but it can also be an opportunity to learn and grow. Building resilience can help you overcome future challenges and achieve your goals. Remember to take care of yourself, seek support, and stay positive.

Conclusion

The Art of Dealing with a Malicious Boss is a comprehensive guide for individuals who find themselves working under a difficult boss. Whether you are dealing with a micromanager, a bully, or someone who is simply difficult to work with, this book provides valuable insights and strategies to help you navigate the situation with grace and professionalism.

Throughout this book, we have explored a wide range of topics, from understanding your boss's motivations and triggers to maintaining your composure in high-pressure situations, building trust and rapport, and protecting yourself in case of legal issues. We have also discussed how to navigate office politics, manage conflicts, provide constructive feedback, and address underperformance, among other important topics.

One of the key themes that emerges from these discussions is the importance of emotional intelligence. The ability to understand and manage your own emotions, as well as those of others, is crucial when dealing with a difficult boss. By developing emotional intelligence, you can remain calm and focused, communicate *effectively, and build positive relationships with others in your workplace.*

Another important theme is the need to take a long-term perspective when dealing with a difficult boss. Rather than simply reacting to each difficult situation as it arises, it is important to think strategically about your career goals and how you can achieve them despite the challenges presented by your boss. This may involve developing new skills, seeking out opportunities for growth and development, and building relationships with allies within your organization.

Of course, there may come a point when it is simply not possible to continue working under a difficult boss. In such cases, it is important to know when it is time to move on and how to do so in a way that is both professional and effective. This may involve finding a new job or career path, building resilience, and learning from your experiences in order to grow and develop as a professional.

Throughout this book, we have also emphasized the importance of seeking help and support when dealing with a difficult boss. This may involve speaking with a trusted mentor or friend, seeking out professional counseling or coaching, or even consulting with a lawyer if legal issues arise.

Ultimately, the key message of this book is that it is possible to thrive in a difficult work environment, even when dealing with a malicious boss. By remaining calm, professional, and strategic, you can not only survive, but also grow and develop as a professional. We hope that the insights and strategies presented in this book will prove valuable to anyone dealing with a difficult boss, and we wish you the best of luck in your career journey.